A Forward-Thinking Guide to Bounce Back, *Bigger* and *Better*

DR. IBORO UDOH

Copyright © 2022 Dr. Iboro Udoh

All rights reserved. No part of this publication may be reproduced, distributed, or transmitted in any form or by any means, including photocopying, recording, or other electronic or mechanical methods, without the prior written permission of the publisher, except in the case of brief quotations embodied in critical reviews and certain other noncommercial uses permitted by copyright law.

ISBN Hardcover: 978-1-63616-107-5
ISBN Paperback: 978-1-63616-119-8
ISBN eBook: 978-1-63616-108-2

Published, Cover Illustration & Edited by
Opportune Independent Publishing Company

Printed in the United States of America

For permission requests, write to the publisher, addressed "Attention: Permissions Coordinator" to the address below.
info@opportunepublishing.com
www. opportunepublishing.com

If you would like to contact Dr. Udoh, go to www.iboroudoh.com

This Book is a Gift

FROM

_____

TO

_____

DATE

_____

ON THE OCCASION OF

_____

_____

This book is dedicated to "The Almighty God," the one who continues to cause all things to work together for my good and to those who believe He can do the same for them. God is always God, and God is always good! He can turn your obstacles into opportunities.

CONTENTS

Foreword	9
Quote	11
Introduction	15
01. God Is The God Of The Rebound	21
02. Get Up And Get It	27
03. Are You Ready To Rebound?	35
04. You've Got The Power	43
05. A Mind Shift	49
06. A Setback Is Not The End Of Your Story	57
07. You Are Not Defined By Your Mistakes	63
08. The Right Mindset	71
09. A Judger Or A Learner?	77
10. The Right Mix	83
11. Learn From It	89
12. The Power Of Mentors	95
Acknowledgments	99
About The Author	101

REBOUND

FOREWORD

Rebound is a deep expression of a classical revelation from the heart of an emerging author who combines intellectual capacity with spiritual sagacity to present her generation with an anchor of hope and a pivot of change in today's world of fear, defeat, and uncertainty.

Many years ago, I watched this vessel of gold, Mrs. Iboro Udoh, PhD, an Associate Professor, pass through humble days of tutorship and years of mentorship to this moment that I can say that God Almighty is showing her forth as a pathfinder to her generation and a candlelight to her acquaintances through this book, *Rebound*.

In this book, the author is simply summarizing that God can turn your mistakes and setbacks into learning tools if you have the right mindset, great mentors, and the readiness and willingness to get up and get it.

The contents are intriguing; the demonstrations are exciting. I am therefore compelled, with all sense of humility and with all glory to God, who reveals these secrets to man, to recommend this book to all who are ready to turn their lives around and impact their generation positively.

Happy reading. Please enjoy.
Be of good cheer!

— Bishop Dr. Emmah Gospel Isong JP
International President, Christian Central Chapel International, Calabar, Nigeria
National Publicity Secretary, Pentecostal Fellowship of Nigeria - PFN
Founder, Remedy For Victims of Religious Persecution & Discrimination

QUOTE

"A courageous person is not one without mistakes, but one who holds his/her head and standards high despite their mistakes and turns his/her obstacles into opportunities. He/She sees the light at the end of the tunnel, becomes that light, and then encourages others to do the same."

— **DR. IBORO UDOH**

REBOUND

Introduction

REBOUND

Anything worth doing or having demands that we move forward in new directions, make bold moves, and take courageous risks. Robert Kennedy said that some "see things as they are and say, 'Why?'"—I envision things that never were and say, "Why not?"

If we must enjoy the next chapter of our lives, we might as well take bold steps, release, and let go of our fears, knowing full well that with God, we can bounce back bigger and better from life's challenges and setbacks.

We all have challenges and setbacks, and sometimes, they are bad, but a setback can become a stepping stone to success. Peter's life in Luke 5:1-11 illustrates this reality. Can you recall the story of Peter and his friends? They went fishing all night but caught nothing. How disappointing this must have been! Peter's specialty was fishing, and yet, his solid boat, high-quality net, and knowledge failed him. Peter must have been discouraged and felt like giving up. However, as Peter and his friends were washing their nets on the seashore, Jesus Christ walked to them and requested to use Peter's boat. Peter let Him use his boat, and they launched out a little way from the shore. Jesus used Peter's boat as a platform to speak to as many as gathered to hear His word. After addressing the crowd, Jesus took Peter and his friends to fish. He instructed them to launch out into the deep water and let down the nets. Peter and his friends never knew they were about to experience a rebound. As most people do, Peter began to remind Jesus of how hard they had worked and caught nothing all night. Then, Peter quickly came to his senses. He obeyed and let down his nets. What happened next dazed them. They had a mind-blowing catch that broke their nets. Simply put, they had a rebound. What they had missed or lost, they got back.

Do you know that sometimes in life, we may give something our best shot, but still come up five feet short? Life can be challenging, and you may be tempted to throw in the towel.

What does this story teach us about setbacks and failure? You can rebound if you take small, but meaningful, steps in the right direction.

As we compare the two scenarios, we see the first scenario, where the disciples had worked all night and caught nothing. In the second scenario, they went with Jesus some minutes later, and caught more than they had imagined. What changed? It was the same lake, the same boat, the same net, and the same people fishing.

It is important to realize that God is interested in your rebound; He's not interested in seeing you fail. Remember, it is more important to do something, though imperfectly, than to do nothing perfectly. Sometimes, we just must keep trying different things until we get it right. If we are passionate, committed, and believe in ourselves, anything is possible.

It all starts when we wake up every day. Do you know that God has given each of us a gift of 24 hours, 1,440 minutes, and more than 86,000 seconds? Before rushing off to start our day, do we pause and think about this? It is always the right time to get up and get whatever we may have lost in the past. Now is the right time to rebound from that setback, mistake, or challenge. Shake it off—the discouragement, fear, and failure—and bounce back, bigger and better.

Regardless of where we have been, we can turn the page and begin again.

Rather than attend pity parties, make the most use of all you've been through. Turn those obstacles into opportunities of growth. Doing this takes optimism, courage, resilience, confidence, and tenacity. Remember, you are the author of the story of your life, and if you really want the next chapter of your life to be your best chapter, you must put things into perspective and be optimistic, knowing that beyond the clouds, the sun is still shining.

With this mindset, we can face each challenge, mistake, or setback and bounce back from it stronger, bigger, and better.

Do not shrink from your challenges or setbacks, or look at what you have lost or missed. Will you run or rise from it? Look at what you still have and use it as a springboard to grow and become all that God wants you to be.

What is an author without a reader? What is the reader without the text? As I put paper and pen together to create this piece, I am reminded to work in the readers' shoes. Each chapter in this book highlights the powerful keys that can unlock your potential and create a culture where you are able to pick yourself up and thrive despite your challenges.

For everyone reading this book, **remember that a setback is not the end of your story.**

Congratulations for picking up an intellectually and thought-provoking read. This is a book about hope and the invitation God gives us to rise above every obstacle. It is a call to push you to a place where occasions rise to you.
You've been warned. It will be hard to put down once you start reading. So, get your coffee or tea ready to enjoy this hard-to-put-down read.

Chapter 1

REBOUND

GOD IS THE GOD OF THE REBOUND

God is the God of the rebound. No matter the setbacks, mistakes, or challenges you are going through, remember that God is always God, and God is always good. He has an exit plan for every challenge you may be facing. He can turn things around and give you a fresh start just like that.

God has given us the freedom to climb any peak and chase any dream. With more resilience, you can boldly explore all that God has for you and go wherever your dream takes you.

Who would not like to bounce back bigger and better from that setback, and live a life that is above and beyond the ordinary: full of purpose, passion, and power? Absolutely none.

When that difficult season descends on us, sometimes, we are there for a short time that seems like forever. Sometimes, the end seems to be nowhere in sight.

At this point, we hardly remember that it's only a bend, not the end. We often ponder and wonder how we'd ever get to a place of recovery from setbacks, mistakes, and obstacles.

The good news is that God offers us His presence during the storm, but we need to accept Him as our Lord and Savior.

I once heard a story of a lady who was a committed Christian and had dedicated her life to serving God and people, but her husband was not a Christian. She prayed and talked to him about it, yet the more she tried to talk to him about having a personal relationship with God and letting Him be his Lord, the more obstinate he became. One day, they were both invited to a baby christening service, and the preacher, a very charismatic and eloquent pastor who always had a good response whenever he preached, made a call for people to step forward, accept Christ into their hearts, and dedicate their lives to God.

Her husband enjoyed the message so much, and to her amazement, he stepped forward to accept the Lord into his life. She was so excited! As the preacher began to explain what dedication meant, the man quickly stepped aside, went back to his seat as fast as he could, and told his wife, "Do you know what? I almost surrendered my life to Jesus Christ."

The wife replied, "Oh, no, you can never go wrong allowing Jesus Christ to come into your heart. You would be making the greatest mistake of your life if you don't accept Him."

This hilarious story is a reminder that we all need a personal relationship with God through Jesus Christ. Without Him, we can do nothing. He has the best rebound plan!

God is in the business of giving fresh starts to people. He gives hope to the hopeless, help to the helpless, and direction to the directionless. Even when things look bleak, keep looking. There is light at the end of the tunnel, if only you can persevere a little longer. If your dreams have seemingly gone up in smoke, don't count God out of the equation.

> **With Him, you can bounce back from any storm—bigger and better, and with a bang!**

NOW is the moment to break down walls that impede your confidence and resilience.

To those who have lost their drive at these precarious moments, do not give up. Remember that difficult trials can challenge our faith or make the skeptic within wonder whether God exists. As we surrender ourselves to God, it's never too late for Him to help us to rise from the storm. Our circumstances cannot inhibit God from fulfilling His plans and purposes for our lives. Remember, a confident and resilient person who has God on his or her side can pick themselves up despite their mistakes and setbacks, knowing that they can rise and shine.

Chapter 2

REBOUND

GET UP AND GET IT

Everybody needs a rebound! Rebounding is a calm skill that requires patience to learn and master in the game of basketball. It empowers basketball players to gain crucial positioning under the basket, thus allowing them to outperform or overtake ostensibly taller and stronger opponents. A rebound gives an individual, whether as a player in a basketball game, a professional in an organization, an entrepreneur, or a student, extra chances and unrestricted opportunities to get back what was lost or missing.

Despite our setbacks and mistakes, we can bounce back bigger and better if we reflect on what practices to keep, what to leave behind, and what to build in our journey. For instance, in a school setting, to ensure that students bounce back after setbacks and mistakes, educators need to address the collective experiences students may have had in order to determine practices that were stressful, and those that were helpful.

> **In an age widely defined by change, disruption, and uncertainty, two things are certain: setbacks and mistakes!**

Who agrees we share this in common? In life, there will be winds that blow. Sometimes, winds of difficulty are brought on by our own decisions, or winds of adversity blow due to circumstances we never saw coming. Yet, ultimately, we can bounce back bigger and better.

Rebounding is key to winning and becoming successful in life.

Have you ever wondered why professional athletes are experts at bouncing back from a loss? They can put a loss behind them so quickly and move forward with the same confidence and resolve they had prior to the loss.

To examine the area of resilience more closely, we need to ask ourselves this question: *Why are professional athletes experts at bouncing back?* The answer is simple: They cultivate a habit of accepting the loss, shaking it off, and moving forward towards a tangible process. Is it easy for them to shake it off and move on? Absolutely not!

They have a "get up and get it" attitude. They prepare

themselves for a rebound by practicing skills and drills. Just as professional athletes take time out to train and practice their skills and drills, the big question is: How are you improving yourself so you can bounce back bigger and better after a setback? We need to take time out to invest in our personal development. These include self-improvement activities that develop our capabilities and potential; that enhance our quality of life and the actualization of our dreams. Self-development ensures that we are well equipped with social, emotional, and practical skills required to rebound from setbacks and challenges. These skills further build confidence and resilience, and enable us to bounce back from challenges in a bigger and better way.

Make no mistake—the fear of making mistakes is deeply ingrained in our consciousness. It takes being intentional to get up. No one accidentally gets up. Simply put, getting up is a conscious, well-thought-out decision that requires effort. To move forward from any setback or challenge, whether as a CEO, pastor, student, entrepreneur, or professional, we need some level of assertiveness, resilience, and confidence.

How do we cope with setbacks or mistakes in our daily lives?

We can start by making the most of these three: resolve, attitude, and adaptability.

No one can rebound without a resolve or determination to consistently move forward in the direction of their dream.

A positive attitude makes rebounding doable. Developing an optimistic attitude that easily shakes off setbacks or mistakes is what I call the "I can bounce back" attitude. This is the right kind of attitude. It energizes us to put on a positive front: standing tall with our shoulders back, moving forward with the routines of our daily life, and persevering towards our goals despite setbacks or mistakes. This attitude ultimately improves our confidence and optimism. It also causes us to speak positive words of affirmation, which looks like this: "I can do this. I've got this. I have what it takes. I am moving forward. I can come back strong."

> **Remember, you must convince yourself before you can convince anybody else.**

The ability to adapt to the disruptions of life is key in bouncing back.

As we all know, in a basketball game, it is common for the ball to bounce off the net. But guess what? With a rebound, a player gets the ball back after he misses. Gaining possession of the ball ultimately helps a team win the game. Consequently, a rebound guarantees an increase in value and strength following a decline, setback, or adversity. The concept of a rebound powerfully demonstrates that it is possible to bounce back from any challenge or mistake stronger, bigger, and better if we are determined.

It is a common consensus that setbacks and mistakes are an important part of the learning process. Rather than give up in frustration, we should work constructively to understand how and why the setback or mistake happened, then figure out the best approach or strategy to solve the problem. This, by far, stays with us better than if we do nothing about it.

We can no longer sit down on the sidelines of life's challenges and obstacles, waiting for a time when our lives will be free of challenges. And then, one day, it suddenly dawns on us that these obstacles, setbacks, and challenges we face are called LIFE.

What is certain is that we all have setbacks. What is uncertain is whether, and how much, we learn from them. In most cases, setbacks are more often punished, rather than seen as opportunities for growth.

A rebound is the only way a player in a basketball game, an entrepreneur, a leader, an employee in an organization, or a student in school can recover and prove their worth through extra chances and unrestricted opportunities.

REBOUND

Chapter 3

REBOUND

ARE YOU READY TO REBOUND?

There is always a second chance. It's called a rebound. The big question then is, *are you ready to rebound?* A rebound can be compared to an extra chance at doing something or having something bigger and better. It is an opportunity to recover and prove your worth—not for the applause of others, but for yourself.

Rebounding is a key skill that we all need in order to get back all we had lost or missed. It requires that we have the following attributes:
1. Assertiveness
2. Positioning
3. Tenacity

A combination of assertiveness, right positioning, and tenacity is essential if we are to bounce back bigger, stronger, and better.

How do we pick off all the loose balls that come

from unexpected challenges and setbacks?

> **We must be prepared so that we can be ready.**

First, we must be confident and anticipate that the ball will come off the rim. Anticipating setbacks and mistakes is not planning to fail; rather, refusing to acknowledge and prepare for them is failing to plan. Mistakes could be compared to preparing to miss shots. A good way to get out of the habit of watching shots before going in for the rebound is to always think that you will miss every shot. This way of thinking does not make us a pessimist, rather it enables us to think about where the shot will come off the rim, so we are well prepared.

Second, we must be well-positioned to gain possession of the ball. This means we must be aligned with practices that improve success. Third, we must be determined, ready, and willing to bounce back bigger and better.

So, the big question is, *how can we bounce back?*

Individuals who want to bounce back bigger and better must have a rebounding motto that reads, "The ball belongs to me, and come rain or shine, I am going to have it."

A person's mental outlook is critical to rebound. Just like in a basketball game, we need the right frame of mind when going for the ball. We must be determined to do our best to get the ball. This mental and physical toughness pays off in the long run.

Of utmost importance is that *you are not your mistake!* God can turn the biggest mistakes of our life into the greatest miracles. No matter how impossible your situation may seem, God can turn it around. Are you ready?

Regardless of the obstacles you're facing, God can redeem even your darkest moments and turn your obstacles into opportunities for growth. Despite life's challenges, you can surge forward and become a winner. Are you ready?

All who have met with setbacks and challenges must be equipped with confidence, independence, and skill to both navigate and learn from it.

Learning from setbacks and mistakes is a process that takes time. If they are learned from and responded to, setbacks and mistakes are powerfully great.

In recent times, we all have been reminded of how our world has significantly changed, and we've had to rebound from the COVID-19 pandemic. We've had to deviate from what we had known as normal, and for a while, we embraced and acclimated to the "new normal." Literally, everyone and everywhere was affected negatively. Why? The answer is simple: We were not ready for the pandemic.

For a period, families were separated from their loved ones, and certain members of the family had to take on new roles. Education was hit hard as students were pulled and stretched in different ways. They had to hold it together, but under a great deal of pressure. As expected, mistakes and setbacks were encountered due to the abrupt disruption in such critical time. No one was ready for the sudden change. While some faced traumatic experiences during this period and recovered, others did not.

Just as we had to bounce back from the COVID-19 pandemic, we also must bounce back from setbacks and challenges that life throws at us so that we can live successful and significant lives.

Wait a minute—what criteria must be met so that setbacks lead to success and not to dead ends? It's simple: We must be tired of losing and be ready to rebound.

It is completely normal to feel overwhelmed when faced with setbacks. However, you must be ready and willing to get to a place where you no longer rise to the occasion, but occasions rise to you.

A good number of people have challenges and barriers that they must overcome to succeed in life. Some have more than others. Since we all are prone to setbacks, it is important for us to recognize and identify them early and start planning the path that we must take to ensure we recover all we've lost or missed in the past.

REBOUND

Chapter 4

REBOUND

YOU'VE GOT THE POWER

You have the power to bounce back. Better believe it! The journey of life can be an uphill task, full of curves, loops, and speed bumps, and we may even have several flats along the road. Thus, we need confidence and resilience to get back up from whatever odds may have been against us.

Life can be compared to a school with classes, where we learn life's lessons. Simply put, everyone is a student of life because we keep learning every day! As we journey through life, where we find ourselves at any point in time can be used as a learning experience. What matters is how we go through and grow through the different classes. Thus, we need to make good use of the totality of our life's experiences—the good, the bad, and the ugly—to sail smoothly through the journey of life.

Every day of our lives, whether we are aware of it or not, we are constantly learning from our experiences, environments, and events around us. Learning goes beyond academic work and includes the gaining of any knowledge that can give us instructions on how to live. These include a well-defined focus on communication, relationship, collaboration, and everything in between.

What would you say if you were told that next to the home or church, the power you need to become the best God wants you to become is embedded in the totality of your life experiences, setbacks, challenges? Many would probably shake their heads in disbelief and point to powerful places like the top Fortune 500 companies, the Presidential Villa, the White House, and the United States Capitol. As powerful as each of these places are, none can be compared to the power you have to change your life. The power to bounce back from anything lies within us. Know how to use it!

Yes, God strengthens us to do all things, but we have a significant role to play. When we believe the word of God, "I can do all things through Christ, who strengthens me," we will bounce back from anything. Think about this: The ultimate rebound of Jesus Christ from the dead embraces all our personal rebounds.

In life, we have a list of the things we would like to accomplish.

Interestingly, setbacks and mistakes unquestionably will not be on that list. This is because we are a generation of people who are petrified of having challenges or barriers, making mistakes, failing, or even sitting with the discomfort of not knowing something for a few minutes.

> **The bottom line is this: If we are afraid of setbacks and mistakes, it means we are afraid of trying something new, being innovative, or thinking in a different way.**

For instance, many people are terrified to raise their hands when they do not know the answer to a question or the solution to a problem. Most times, their response to a difficult problem is to ask others rather than try different solutions that, though may be incorrect, will be a great learning experience.

Essentially, most people view success in life as having all their needs met with all the good things of life at their beck and call. If needs are all that matter in life, then setbacks and mistakes play no positive role, but we all know they play a significant role in everyone's life. We grow through setbacks and life's challenges. Life is not balanced without setbacks, mistakes, and challenges.

It is important to note that mistakes are only valuable if we believe that the process of learning, which unavoidably must include the process of making mistakes, is just as important as getting the answers right.

We must begin to rethink our approach to the process of learning from setbacks and mistakes. Facing setbacks and making mistakes is not failure; rather, it is a pointer to what still needs to be learned. How about that?

Chapter 5

REBOUND

A MIND SHIFT

What is life without learning? What is learning without setbacks? What are setbacks without a rebound? Absolutely nothing!

It is clear that no one likes setbacks or mistakes. However, the reality is that we all have met with both and must learn from them. This is crucial if we are to become resilient learners and risk-takers, who accept the uncertainty of not knowing everything.

All through life, a setback indicates the possibility of achieving below the expectation of others, since we all assume that good people hardly have setbacks. In our homes, setbacks and mistakes lead to reproofs. It is a consensus that good children should always follow the rules. In the workplace, mistakes have severe consequences because employers believe that good workers must get it right the first time. However, we must remember that when individuals are marked down for making mistakes, these individuals often stumble upon great innovations.

> **We need to embrace the possibility of shifting the prism at least slightly so that we see mistakes and setbacks in a different way, rather than things to be dreaded.**

They should be viewed as inevitable, yet helpful parts of learning.

Building this kind of confidence is not easy. I have observed firsthand the challenges individuals experience in leadership training sessions, where questions are projected on slides, and participants hold up their answers. Here is what happens all the time, without fail: The first question is somewhat easy, and all participants quickly and confidently hold up their letter choice. As more intricate questions are posed, they start to shy away from holding their choices high, shuffle through their letter choices as if in deep thought, or skim at the choices that other participants are selecting.

At the end of the sessions, I direct their attention to this behavior to dissuade them from focusing on mistakes; rather, encourage them to focus on learning from them. Thus, a paradigm shift is necessary to enhance learning and growth.

We need a mind shift in the way we perceive the

setbacks and mistakes of others. Identifying the rationale behind setbacks is the right thing to do, rather than playing the blame game. The focus should be on the positive effects so we can use them as a springboard, turning them to something good.

The whole process of mind shift hinges on us. When we are more empathetic and accommodating towards others who are faced with setbacks and mistakes, they are more motivated to learn and grow from them, as we all do.

A mind shift is critical! No day or person is perfect. However, we all can look within and do better. Where will we start? Let's start with positivity!

An essential component of this effort would be to cultivate an inclusive and enabling attitude that sends a clear message to all: You are important, we value you, we believe in your ability to do great things, and we will support you to do more than you think possible, despite your setbacks.

We must begin to embrace a positive attitude that builds our confidence and energizes us to bounce back from our challenges. Conversely, a negative attitude undermines everything. Having the best strategies in place while neglecting the right attitude creates a recipe for mediocrity. Thus, a mind shift is the key ingredient in the recipe for a successful rebound.

If you think it is important to have a mind shift, that can begin with YOU. Yes, it can begin with just one person. It can be as simple as sending notes of encouragement to individuals who struggle or creating a bright and cheerful bulletin board that celebrates the achievements of students or employees. We can also offer positive words to people we meet daily to brighten their days. Taking a minute to ask another person how their day went goes a long way.

We need to be prepared to create a positive culture by embracing a radical change in the way things have been done in the past. A change in our thinking, attitude, mindset, and behavior is needed to achieve a positive culture where individuals can bounce back bigger and better from any setback or mistake.

To build a strong community, we must intentionally solicit the contributions of mentors and coaches to empower and re-engage unplugged people who have lost their drive in pursuing their goals in the best possible manner, especially when they are faced with setbacks.

Remember, no one starts out as a gold medalist, not even an exceptional athlete who has an abundance of natural talent. An athlete develops into a superstar through hard work, practice, and learning from mistakes. This is true of top performers in every field where excellence is expected.

A great example is when we learn to ride a bicycle. We make mistakes along the way as we figure out the proper balance and speed needed to keep the bike steady and moving. Do you remember the first time you rode a bicycle? Can you relive the excitement of riding, and the sense of accomplishment you felt? Now, step back. How many times did you fall off the bike before that first ride? Gradually, with more practice, you eventually rode with confidence.

Why is it so hard to replicate that process in our homes, families, churches, schools, and organizations? Having worked with people of various age groups, I have rarely seen any of them welcome their setbacks or mistakes, let alone display some willingness to learn from them. What prevents people from embracing and learning from them? How can we create environments that encourage them to do so? We can start in our own little way.

Certainly, we must hold ourselves accountable to a significant level of competence. A great way to meet that expectation is by sharing our own challenges, setbacks, and lessons learned with others. We need to be courageous enough to do this and encourage others to bounce back bigger and better.

We live in a society that focuses so much on what goals were not met and what went wrong.

How often have we yelled at our kids for spilling a cup of milk or accidentally throwing a plate in the trash? Why do we correct children more often for words they bungle than the sentences they can read perfectly? We need to move away from the practice of throwing stones rather than applaud. A mind shift is imperative!

REBOUND

Chapter 6

REBOUND

A SETBACK IS NOT THE END OF YOUR STORY

Having a setback is part of life. Making mistakes is part of the learning process. Through setbacks and mistakes, problems are solved. Therefore, encouraging people to come up with innovative strategies to remedy setbacks supports both growth and success. Innovation develops better when individuals are given the space to make mistakes. Many inventions were created through experimentation and by mistake. Freedom is not complete until one has the freedom to make mistakes and embrace setbacks.

Why, then, do people frown at those who make mistakes and face setbacks? Think about this! Have you ever taken a guess? Whether you guessed right or wrong, guessing is useful, as it gives you the ability to recall information, even when the guess is wrong. No single action has done more damage to people than the crippling effect of facing setbacks and making mistakes. People often feel stuck when they make mistakes, and this often keeps them from pursuing promising opportunities. Furthermore, the fear of making more mistakes inhibits them from taking courageous risks that could lead them to bounce back bigger and better.

It is not the end of your story when you face challenging situations.

> **We must learn to stand tall with our shoulders back, move forward with our pursuits, and persevere towards our dreams and goals, despite setbacks.**

Most times, mistakes are meant to protect us from danger in the future, though they end up as traps that keep us from succeeding. Mistakes have a humbling effect.

Not all mistakes are necessarily bad. Before anyone can completely conquer mistakes, they must first understand why mistakes happen and how mistakes work to their advantage. For instance, mistakes that are a near miss can help one learn better than if none were made at all. These near misses can serve as stepping stones to rebound from challenges.

Have you ever witnessed a situation where you thought you were invincible? Certainly, you can say that these are the moments when you felt small, and anxiety enveloped you. These defining moments often serve as a reminder that we are emphatically not invincible.

No one is exempt from mistakes. Mistakes keep us on our toes. For instance, an employee who has the tendency of running behind schedule when handling projects and never meets deadlines, whether for genuine reasons or due to carelessness, sooner or later develops a plan that keeps him or her alert, prepared, and ready to respond better when faced with seemingly difficult tasks. Who agrees?

We must allow and make room for setbacks and mistakes. Here is a good example: If you want to test a person's understanding of a subject, just asking them for answers or using multiple-choice questions will not provide insight into the reasons for their mistakes.

At the end of the day, people who allow and make room for mistakes understand that resiliency is central to both learning and growth. Individuals who are resilient can rebound from adversity and resist being pulled into hopelessness by difficult situations. They often develop self-direction, problem-solving capabilities, resilience, competence, and are ultimately more productive in the world around them.

REBOUND

Chapter 7

REBOUND

YOU ARE NOT DEFINED BY YOUR MISTAKES

For anyone feeling disappointed, beaten down, or like a failure because of the choices you've made or circumstances you've found yourself in, remember: You are not defined by your mistakes—you are defined by God. In Psalms 139:13-14, the Bible states, "For you created my inmost being: you knit me together in my mother's womb. I praise you because I am fearfully and wonderfully made; your works are wonderful; I know that full well."

A mistake is not your identity. It is logical that people who have experienced setbacks often feel defeated in every sense of the word. They often say, "My experience has deserted me. My dream career has eluded me. My intelligence has failed me. I cannot believe that the brilliant identity I had been bragging about has dramatically vanished before my eyes. I have not just made a mistake; I am a mistake. I have no idea how I would ever recover and live any sort of a meaningful life moving forward."

Interestingly, this is how setbacks and mistakes play out in our lives. Many people often feel that they will never come out of their funk. If you are not convinced, think about when you were learning to drive a car for the first time, how you kept missing your way, and how you were convinced the world was coming to an end. Did it? Absolutely not!'

Mistakes are sneaky little liars. When a mistake happens, we forget it is only a temporary situation and it should not define us in any way.

Mistakes are not all bad.

> **The good thing about mistakes is that once you learn from them, you bounce back bigger and better.**

The only bad thing is if you never learn.

The role of everyone in the school called life is to learn, learn, learn… not only from others, but even from our challenges and setbacks.

Setbacks, hurricanes, natural disasters, lockdowns,

and wrecks are some of the unexpected balls life throws at us. From the small crises to the truly terrible, we have seen it all and must be ready for anything. Setbacks and mistakes are transformative. Are we ever prepared? No one thinks about a rebounding strategy at the forefront of their plans when they set out on a task until they are faced with the unexpected, the need for adaptability, and the possible need for a rebound.

For instance, no one was prepared for the COVID-19 pandemic. Many people have had a difficult time adapting to the disruptiveness of their schedules, specifically in the face of the pandemic. Many made numerous mistakes as they struggled to manage their own time. During the pandemic, people who once had a structured schedule had to establish their own routines in the wake of an abrupt and unforeseen increase in independence.

For everyone, including organizations, churches, schools, students, and educators, the virtual learning environment that the pandemic forced us to adopt did not make the shift easier.

Most people were saddled with the task of becoming digital natives, whether they were prepared to or not. Many made massive mistakes navigating this new virtual environment; many had setbacks and could not catch up.

Another hurdle these novel digital natives had to overcome to connect or access learning in this new environment was the extra pressure that holding meetings or classes from the comfort of their home put on them.

Many employees and students had to work through issues with family interferences, time management, prioritization, boundary-setting, and balance. Other barriers included internet connectivity and navigating the unfamiliar terrain of online platforms.

We were all stuck in our homes as we tried to replicate our entire lives from the comfort of our homes and, understandably, it was not a smooth transition. For instance, during this period, employers, employees, students, entrepreneurs, and leaders were inevitably slammed with work. They had a bunch of projects and meetings piled up. Simply put, they were bound to make mistakes, as many found themselves falling behind.

This was a critical time where many needed a strong support system to get on with their lives. Some had no choice but to change their schedules to keep up with their workloads. No better time did we need the help of each other to bounce back than during the pandemic. Surprisingly, during this trying time, countless people bounced back bigger and better.

How did this happen? During this period, people connected with each other and made conscious efforts to stay healthy, and this made them more resilient. Though most people were stressed, this became a good motivator for people to rebound from the pandemic stronger, bigger, and better. The pandemic was a challenging time. Our resilience and rebound from the pandemic further proved that we are not defined by our challenges.

REBOUND

Chapter 8

REBOUND

THE RIGHT MINDSET

Today, due to the fast and evolving twenty-first century, most people have no time to pause for a breath, as they are left to figure things out by themselves. Sometimes, the abruptness of change leaves people not in the right mindset, causing them to sometimes become disorganized, confused, and prone to make mistakes, which may lead to setbacks. Thus, it is safe to say that achieving our goals these days is not easy.

Whether in Africa, the United States, or Asia, people are busy, not necessarily productive. Everyone keeps going, just as the clock does. Today, life is much more complex than it has ever been, and our lives may seem especially challenging, sometimes, due to unforeseen winds. Yet, we must understand that God oversees the winds.

This kind of thinking stretches our understanding and calls us to believe again that God is good and His thoughts for us are good, regardless of what is happening around us. If we are to bounce back and recover all we have lost or missed, we must change our minds and the stigma that is associated with setbacks or mistakes.

We must be assertive and optimistic in developing ourselves until we attain the confidence and resilience required to overcome our barriers.

> **Change needs to start from our minds gradually before proceeding through our entire community.**

It begins with a positive mindset on simple, yet powerful ways that we can be guided when we face setbacks, and how this mindset shift can ultimately stimulate growth in our lives.

The right mindset will make the experience of everyone one of thriving, not just surviving! When we know this, we will know peace. The Bible declares this: All things work together for our good. Having the right mindset requires an intentional and precise tuning of the mind.

Most importantly, as we seek to fulfill our purpose on earth, we must adopt a set of core principles that determine how we operate our lives as we strive for success and significance.

The right mindset embraces failing forward and recognizes that we need a hand to hold us up every step of the way.

How many times have we created an awful mental visualization of ourselves failing before we even took an important step? Whether it is that compelling presentation we must make in front of an audience or the projects we embark on, we tend to envision ourselves having slip-ups and mistakes. In other words, we always anticipate that the first presentation will need some corrections, which explains why we have several drafts or why the execution of that large project may not be seamless.

The stigma against setbacks and mistakes carries over into adulthood, too. Even the most motivated of us do not like setbacks or mistakes. We view them as the hassles or barriers that keep us from reaching our goals as quickly as we had hoped. As inevitable as mistakes are, many of us wish we would simply get it right the first time around. This outlook tends to put more pressure than we can imagine on ourselves by imagining negative outcomes. The truth is that we should never do that again!

The reason we have corrections and revisions is that in life, we must plan for setbacks and mistakes. Simply put, making a mistake only means that you took an action or made a judgment that did not turn out right. See the difference?

How else can you learn about how to handle some situations besides the mistakes you made or the problems you solved? Why do you care that you failed a presentation? After all, you now know exactly what you did wrong, and will never make that mistake again. It is better to deal with mistakes NOW than wait years trying to figure them out.

No matter our age today, we are all growing older every day. This is simply a fact of life. A key factor for thriving in life during the up-and-down season is resilience, the capacity to bounce back from life's challenges. More than ever, we must make up our minds to shake off every difficult experience, stress, or challenge. A person with the right mindset believes this: If I don't give up, I can still flourish and thrive; it's not too late to rise again; I can still recover what I have missed or lost in the past.

Remember that part of rising or bouncing back is developing the grit to keep getting up after every fall. Ultimately, setbacks and mistakes help us find better solutions and are part of the learning process. Rather than feel defeated, we should begin to see the good in a seemingly bad situation and see how we can rise from it, rather than run from it.

Chapter 9

REBOUND

A JUDGER OR A LEARNER?

Life is too short to learn everything the first time. No one is mistake-proof. As we go through life's challenges and setbacks, we are faced with the choice of adopting a learner mindset or a judger mindset. The judger mindset comes quite inherently to us. Everyone tends to judge others, though we also have learner moments.

The learner mindset opens us up to opportunities, while the judger mindset leaves us, at the very least, in an unproductive state. The learner mindset is a choice, while the judger mindset is a reaction to our circumstances. As we aspire to become change agents, it is important to note that we cannot help anyone from a place of judgment. There is a huge difference between having good judgment and being judgmental. Good judgment is vital for all decisions we make in life; however, being judgmental is devastating.

> **We need to desist from the practice of throwing stones at people. Rather, let's learn to take notes and applaud people when they improve or perform well.**

It is important to know that a setback is not a life sentence; it is a learning experience. As stated by Nelson Mandela, "I never lose. I either win or learn."

I reminisce about my experience as a nursing student: In one of my classes in nursing school, the instructor asked us to learn how to check a patient's blood pressure using a manual blood pressure machine and a stethoscope. We did that. Then, the instructor asked us to recheck it so she could confirm whether our results were accurate using her own machine. We had incorrect readings and had to practice for days.

Now, this is the lesson: As a class, we learned a lot about checking a person's blood pressure in that short time from the slip-ups or mistakes we made. The moral of this story is: Do you have the audacity to reassure people that they will come out bigger and better after the setbacks that they will inevitably face?

We must resist the urge to buffer people from challenges or setbacks they face, being aware that there are setbacks and that planning for them does not make one a loser. In fact, this is how we all learn.

When babies learn to walk, they always miss their first step. Their first step is a calculated risk. Remember, only the strong and courageous take risks. Each time the baby lets go while learning to walk, the baby is taking a calculated risk.

> **Each missed step brings the baby closer to their best step.**

Similarly, we all have challenges and barriers we must overcome to succeed. Even the greatest business leaders encounter seasons of setbacks and challenges. Remember: Win or lose, pass, or fail, every moment is a learning experience, not a judging experience.

We need to change our perspective and embrace the learner mindset. The learner mindset is aware of the potential for setbacks and mistakes and seeks to turn them into opportunities for growth. A person with a learner mindset does not see obstacles as failing; rather, they see it as an opportunity to learn and figure out how they can do better.

Our greatest assets are people. However, we need the right kind of people to surround us because these are the ones who we would most likely ask for and receive help from. The right kind of people are the people who help you learn through the storm, not

REBOUND
judge you.

Chapter 10

މREBOUND

THE RIGHT MIX

Mistakes, as we all know, are common. However, rebounding from mistakes is not common. The power of making mistakes and learning from them is underrated.

Interestingly, boosting our confidence is one of the best things that the right mix of people can make happen in our lives.

One of the best ways to bounce back from any setback or mistake is by having the support of the right mix of people.

We all need to embrace the culture of teamwork and collaboration.

> **Any person who wants to do great things must be willing to cultivate and maintain good relationships with the right people.**

Everybody is a student of life because we learn daily from our experiences, our environments, and the events taking place around us. To bounce back from setbacks and mistakes, we need the encouragement and guidance of others who have been through this path.

It is important that we put our relationships before things. Things can be easily replaced—relationships, not so easily! We need to reach out to people and be reachable. We cannot be distant or appear standoffish. It is crucial that we collaborate with others and work with mentors who can guide and encourage us. We need people to learn from, and people who will learn from us. Jesus Christ worked with 12 people who had different personalities. He functioned well with them and accomplished his purpose on earth through them. Had some of us conducted the job interviews, these men wouldn't have made the first cut because of our judgmental attitude towards others. However, Jesus did not judge them; He brought them closer to him so they could learn. He saw their potential and invested in them.

We don't need a whole community to work with; we just need a few committed people who are willing to persevere to see us become better.

Jesus Christ was reachable and accessible. Let's refrain from building castles. Anyone with a superiority complex, who only associates with high-class people, would have succeeded in limiting their opportunities for growth.

We must not get easily tired of people. Rather, we ought to find ways to work with even the most difficult person. That loud person brings something to the table; that sober and calm fellow does, as well. That sociable, all-up-in-your-face friend, and the other shy one—both have something to offer. Deal with each person individually and differently.

The trajectory of our lives can change with the right mix of people we surround ourselves with; people who inspire and motivate us to forge ahead, despite what life throws at us.

With the right mix, a relationship with Jesus Christ, confidence and resilience, you can bounce back, bigger and better. Resilience is the trait of being able to adjust to stressful life changes and bounce back from adversity. God requires that we persevere in the face of setbacks. The Bible says, "Though the righteous fall seven times, they rise again." This scripture demonstrates that when we fall, we need to get up, shake off the dust, learn from it, grow from it, and keep moving. With the right mix, it is possible to thrive and succeed, despite our setbacks.

REBOUND

Chapter 11

REBOUND

LEARN FROM IT

Visualize reassuring an individual to keep trying to solve a problem until they make three mistakes. Also, visualize asking them whether they have made their three mistakes yet! Trust me, if you are not making mistakes, you are not learning—or, at least, you are not learning enough.

The more we face setbacks and mistakes, the more resilient we become, if we learn from them. We all have the capacity to exhibit confidence and resilience when we learn from mistakes.

> **The capability to learn is a skill. The readiness to learn from our mistakes is a choice.**

The Oxford Dictionary defines a mistake as an action or judgment that is misguided or wrong. In other words, mistakes are actions that are incorrect.

How can we turn our mistakes into learning opportunities?

Given the certainty of mistakes, we need to see the positive aspects they offer. For one thing, mistakes are humbling since no one is perfect. Therefore, we need to realize that we can never be perfect. We must also understand that no one gets to their goals instantaneously. The process of reaching our goals often takes a lot of mistakes and loads of practice.

Mistakes also force us to focus on the process, not just the outcome. In other words, sometimes, the process of a journey is as important as the end result. This means that we should not be extremely focused only on getting results by any means necessary.

Sometimes, we have these thoughts going on in their minds when we go through setbacks: "I really am trying my best, but I just keep messing up. I try to fix it myself, but I don't know where to start."

Since we live in a face-paced world, we all have become responsible for so much that there is simply more room for mistakes. However, possessing the confidence and resilience needed to navigate and learn from those mistakes is the pathway to success. When we become aware of our mistakes and our potential for making mistakes, it makes us optimize learning by identifying and finding solutions to our challenges early.

Now, more than ever before, mistakes are an inevitable part of the learning process. Without them, we cannot grow. We grow through them. So, how do we place ourselves in a position where we feel comfortable and confident enough to engage with our mistakes, rather than shy away from them?

Simply put, we need to own our mistakes, analyze them, and take positive steps so we can bounce back bigger and better.

Consequently, we should be comfortable with the fact that we are better through setbacks and mistakes, and from them, we learn what not to do. However, this requires a level of self-confidence, independence, resilience, and competence.

REBOUND

Chapter 12

REBOUND

THE POWER OF MENTORS

So, what is a mentor supposed to do, anyway? If this question has crossed your mind, you are not alone. As you face obstacles along the way, a mentor is a person who inspires you to keep going. A mentor is an experienced leader who provides support, guidance, and encouragement to a mentee. Mentoring means reaching out and taking the time to build positive relationships with people who need your experience and expertise because they are about to tread on a path you have gone through.

A great mentor is there to support you until you become successful and significant. Great mentors are great models. They are great models because they demonstrate to their mentees that they have also faced challenges and setbacks, and they know how to support their mentees until they succeed. They have the capacity to positively influence the lives of others. People rely on mentors for guidance and instruction as they navigate life, their career, business, or education. They educate people on how to utilize opportunities and resources and provide them with the necessary skills to meet their goals. Additionally, they help mentees avoid some of the pitfalls they experienced.

The role of a mentor is more of a calling than a job. It is a relationship. Mentors are practically the most valuable resource anyone can have. Therefore, it is imperative that they adequately engage in self-development practices and put themselves at the top of their to-do lists daily.

Mentors who are competently equipped are in the best position to equip others and properly guide them on their paths to success and significance.

Mentorship is worthwhile because it creates meaningful, sustainable relationships with others who need support to grow. These strong and stable relationships that they build with others are helpful in building the confidence and resilience of those who need a helping hand. A mentor guides rather than judges. They cultivate a safe and trusting relationship, a nonjudgmental attitude, and a life of empathy.

The greatest power of mentors is to inspire people to flourish, despite the odds stacked against them. They have a task of motivating people into becoming forward and critical thinkers.

Mentors have the power to steer people in the right path when and if they face setbacks. These Four As are transformative attributes that great mentors possess:

1. Be Accessible
Mentors who are understanding and accessible make it easier for people to reach out to them for help.

2. Be Approachable
A mentor ought to be a people's person. Simply put, they need to enjoy helping people and talking to them. Mentors who are welcoming and have humorous personalities can positively influence people. Humor has a much more appealing, leveling, and most importantly, encouraging effect on people. The attitude and spirit of a mentor makes it easy for people to talk to them.

A mentor with a playful, yet firm, personality can reduce tensions and create an atmosphere conducive enough for all. It can also offer springboards for people to feel safe enough to share their challenges. This allows them to offer solutions accordingly.

As a mentor, I have had mentees say, "The classes in which I succeed most are the ones where the instructors are humorous, particularly when we make blunders." Ultimately, mentors set the tone for mentees to bounce back when they approach the setbacks of others with a sense of humor. If handled properly, humorous moments can offer springboards for rebounds. Mentors who are accessible and approachable put themselves in the shoes of others and are in the best position to observe their numerous sentiments.

3. Be Accepting

Mentors who accept the unavoidable reality that setbacks happen are more likely to accommodate the setbacks of others and give them permission to do the same. Providing people with hope and optimism is essential. People need to know that they are not alone when they face challenges. However, this can only happen when they are guided by mentors who are accepting, nonjudgmental, and practical.

Mentors regularly assure people that imperfection is a part of living, learning, and growing. Mentors are in the best position to encourage people not to incapacitate themselves in quest of perfection, but to incorporate this reality in such a way that is beneficial to their learning experience.

4. Be an Ally

Alliance works! Great mentors serve as allies, which allows for great teamwork and collaboration. They support others to turn their setbacks into opportunities for growth.

ACKNOWLEDGEMENTS

A huge appreciation to my husband, Engr. Ubong Udoh, for his love, prayers, and unwavering support every step of the way.

I dearly appreciate Ubongabasi and Ubokabasi, my twin sons, for always cheering me on.

I sincerely appreciate my Dad and Mom, Hon. & Mrs. A. A. Eno, for their love, prayers, and immense support.

I deeply appreciate my spiritual parents, Bishop Dr. & Pst. Mgtr. Emmah Isong, for their unflinching support, prayers and care.

Special thanks to the former Chief Judge of AKS, His Lordship, Hon. Justice Godwin Abraham & Dr. Emem Abraham (Associate Professor) for their encouragement.

I want to say a huge thank-you to the Udoh and Eno families for their support and care.

REBOUND

ABOUT THE AUTHOR

Iboro Udoh, PhD is an Associate Professor of Education, USA. She is a "Versatilist, Mentor," Success Coach, Education Advocate, and Influencer who strives to effect positive change in educational climates. She is passionate about empowering women, youths, and students to navigate their path towards success and significance. She strongly believes that education is a powerful tool for transformational leadership. She has used her educational background and expertise to create high impact leadership and social awareness programs to develop and support others.

Since moving to the U.S. from Nigeria, she has established herself as a forward-thinking, American-born, Nigerian-raised lady. In 2017, she launched and expanded her vision in founding The VIP Initiative, a faith-based, non-profit organization committed to empowering all on how to use their Time, Talents, and Treasures (TTT) to become *Very Impactful People* (VIPs). Through this organization, she has supported and impacted others through her involvement in community services that promote and uplift others, such as career fairs, workshops, conferences, and mentoring programs. Her organization, VIP Initiative, partners with several organizations to support underserved communities and underprivileged families.

Dr. Udoh has empowered a community of VIP hopefuls and created a culture of diversity and inclusion for young people of all backgrounds. She has been a Healthcare Administrator for 19 years, as well as a Registered Nurse with advanced clinical skills and experiences, delivering exceptional healthcare for 10 years. Transitioning from the healthcare field to the education field has provided her the opportunity to build a multifaceted skill set, be adaptable, achieve a well-balanced view, and has enabled her to bring different perspectives to projects and approach problem-solving differently.

Dr. Udoh earned her Doctor of Education degree in Executive Educational Leadership from Houston

Christian University, Houston, Texas. Due to her outstanding academic performance, a perfect GPA of 4.0 in her Doctoral Program, and her excellent leadership skills, she was identified by the faculty of the School of Education at HCU as a Top Educator and inducted into the International Honor Society in Education. She was the best graduating student in her doctoral program. She served as the Treasurer of DOCS (Doctoral Organization of Community and Service), Houston Christian University. She earned her Nursing degree in Texas. She received her Master of science degrees in Healthcare Administration and Finance from Houston Christian University, Houston, Texas. She received her Bachelor of Science degree in Biology from Nigeria. Dr. Udoh is currently working on her second Nursing degree.

Dr. Udoh is a member of numerous professional organizations, including Texas Council of Professors of Educational Administration (TCPEA), Texas Association of School Administrators (TASA), American Nurses Association (ANA), Texas Nurses Association (TNA), American College of Healthcare Executives (ACHE), and Healthcare Financial Management Association (HFMA). She has presented at various national and state conferences, universities, and schools in the Houston area, where she has been the guest author/speaker. Her most recent state presentation was at The Texas Council of Professors of Educational Administration (TCPEA) in Austin, Texas.

She is an author of the groundbreaking book, *Ignite,* published in 2017; and her most recent book,

Rebound. She is currently working on publishing articles in educational journals. She has received several awards, including The National Scholars Honor Society Award, The Methodist Hospital Volunteer Services Award, Houston Christian University Doctoral Program Award, Houston Christian University Alumni Award, and others. She was honored at Mading's "Becoming" Women's Conference with "The Outstanding Professional." Dr. Udoh has been featured in *galaTAG Magazine*, *The Pillars Magazine* and the cover story of *The Courageous Woman Magazine*, May 2020. She currently serves as a consultant and has been an excellent resource for women, students, and aspiring leaders.

As an American-born lady with Nigerian roots, she has used her strong heritage to build a thriving career in the healthcare field, while balancing motherhood and a family. Her mental fortitude and determination to be a VOICE, a Very Impactful Person (VIP), allows her to pursue her ever-evolving dreams and write her own life rules. Her greatest watchword is, "Believe in yourself, and people will believe in you." With this resilient and persistent mindset, she believes that she and anyone can do anything. In her words, "being a VIP is an inside job. You must see yourself as successful, wanted, important, relevant, and a difference maker, before people can see that in you."

She loves putting smiles on people's faces and has gained a reputation for spicing up any environment she walks into and for always being optimistic. Dr.

Udoh and her husband, Engr. Ubong Udoh, live in Texas with their teenagers.

TO CONTACT THE AUTHOR
Email: vipinitiative2020@gmail.com
www.IboroUdoh.com

Social Media Handles:
www.facebook.com/vipiboro
Instagram: @vipiboro
Twitter: @vipiboro

REBOUND

EVERYBODY NEEDS A REBOUND

We all know what it feels like to have setbacks, challenges, and life not working out as we had hoped. We all know what it's like to long for something more, something bigger, and something better. *Rebound* dares all to bounce back from setbacks or challenges. It offers hope and encouragement to anyone who has met with obstacles or mistakes, whether in their life, faith, profession, or education, to become forward-thinkers by being more resilient in turning their setbacks to opportunities for growth. *Rebound* illustrates to readers how worthwhile their effort is and how their competence improves when they are assertive and well positioned, with a resolve to bounce back bigger and better.

REBOUND

www.ingramcontent.com/pod-product-compliance
Lightning Source LLC
Chambersburg PA
CBHW071904070526
44583CB00016B/1833